JEFFERSON

FISHER

"THE ART OF INFLUENCE"

"Mastering Communication, Leadership, and Persuasion in the Modern Age"

ZAHRA REHAN

Contents

INTRODUCTION

In an era where words hold more power than ever before, few individuals have mastered the art of communication with the precision, charisma, and unwavering confidence of Jefferson Fisher. A name that resonates with authority, intellect, and unshakable composure, Fisher has transformed the way people navigate conflict, command attention, and wield the force of their voice. His journey is not one of mere rhetoric but of profound understanding—of human nature, of persuasion, and of the silent battles that rage in every conversation. He is not just a lawyer, not just a speaker; he is a force, an architect of influence whose impact extends far beyond the courtroom and into the psyche of anyone who has ever sought to be heard.

The world is a battlefield of ideas, where the unprepared are drowned out by the louder, the quicker, the more articulate. Fisher understands this better than most. He has built his reputation not on aggression or intimidation, but on a mastery of poise, a strategic mind that calculates every word before it leaves his lips. To watch him speak is to witness a symphony of control—his tone, his timing, his body language, all harmonizing to create an irresistible force of persuasion. He doesn't just talk; he commands. He doesn't just respond; he disarms. And in doing so, he leaves an indelible mark on those who listen.

His influence is not confined to the walls of a courtroom. In a time where digital platforms shape public discourse, where the lines between professional and personal blur, Fisher has carved a space for himself as a modern mentor. Through screens and stages, he teaches the masses how to keep their composure, how to harness the power of pause, how to turn the tide of any argument without raising their voice. His methods are not about domination but about precision. He is not in the business of proving others wrong—he is in the business of making them listen.

But who is the man behind the influence? What life experiences forged the wisdom he so effortlessly dispenses? Beneath the polished presence and controlled cadence is a story—one of struggle, of refinement, of relentless pursuit. A story that begins not with the accolades or the viral moments, but with the trials that shaped his philosophy. The power he wields today is not something he was simply born with; it was earned, sculpted through moments of doubt, through failures that taught him resilience, through battles—both legal and personal—that refined his understanding of human nature. His is not a story of entitlement but of evolution, a transformation fueled by an insatiable hunger to master the most powerful weapon in existence: words.

To understand Jefferson Fisher is to understand the very mechanics of influence itself. His journey is not just one of personal triumph but a blueprint for anyone who seeks to be more than just a voice lost in the noise. His mastery of persuasion is not some elusive gift but a skill—a skill that can be studied, learned, and applied by those willing to embrace its power. Through his life, his work, and his teachings, he has unveiled the hidden architecture of effective communication, offering the world a new way to navigate conflict, command respect, and reshape the conversations that define our lives.

His legacy is still unfolding, his influence still expanding. But one truth remains steadfast: Jefferson Fisher is not merely a communicator. He is a strategist of speech, a tactician of tone, a sculptor of influence. And in a world that thrives on the ability to persuade, his journey is one worth dissecting, understanding, and—most importantly—learning from.

CHAPTER 01

Early Life and Influences

Before Jefferson Fisher became a master of persuasion, before the courtroom victories and the commanding presence that made him a force to be reckoned with, he was a boy navigating the world with an insatiable curiosity. The journey of a man who would one day wield words like weapons did not begin in the grandeur of legal institutions or the echoes of debate halls. It began in the quiet moments of observation, in the subtle exchanges of everyday life, in the way he learned—long before he ever knew he was learning—that influence was not just about speaking, but about listening.

Fisher was born into an environment where communication was both a necessity and an art form. Conversations at the dinner table were never merely about recounting the day; they were intricate dances of wit, persuasion, and negotiation. Words were currency, and their value depended on how effectively they were used. He watched as family members navigated disagreements with carefully chosen phrases, as his elders asserted authority not with volume but with calculated pauses, as his peers struggled to find footing in the chaotic symphony of human interaction. He absorbed it all, internalizing the unwritten rules of influence long before he understood their significance.

Unlike many who stumble upon their strengths later in life, Fisher showed an early affinity for articulation. While other children focused on memorizing facts for school, he was more intrigued by the way those facts were presented. He noticed that a well-told story held more power than a simple recitation of events. He saw how teachers commanded attention with the rise and fall of their tone, how some students naturally led groups while others followed without question. He dissected these dynamics, storing away each observation like a craftsman collecting tools for a masterpiece yet to be built.

His formative years were filled with moments that sharpened his instincts. A casual debate over playground rules became a lesson in negotiation. An argument with a friend taught him the cost of misplaced words. A disagreement with a teacher showed him the delicate balance between defiance and diplomacy. Every interaction was a classroom, every experience a stepping stone toward mastery.

But influence is not just learned; it is shaped by those who leave their mark along the way. Fisher was fortunate to have mentors—figures who recognized the raw potential in him and nurtured it. Teachers who challenged him to think critically, to see beyond the surface of an argument. Coaches who drilled into him the importance of discipline and strategy, showing him that victory was not always about brute force but about knowing when to strike and when to step back. Even moments of failure became profound lessons, each one refining his understanding of human nature and the power of communication.

As he grew older, his awareness deepened. He began to understand that words could be wielded like instruments—

capable of building, of destroying, of shifting tides in an instant. He saw how authority figures controlled rooms with nothing more than a commanding presence, how leaders inspired movements not with orders but with carefully chosen phrases that resonated with their audience. He studied history, drawn not just to the events themselves but to the speeches that had shaped them, to the voices that had turned tides and redefined narratives.

His adolescence was not without its struggles. Like any young mind eager to test its capabilities, he faced moments of overconfidence, instances where his sharp tongue cut deeper than intended. But with every misstep, he recalibrated. He learned that persuasion was not about overpowering but about guiding, that true influence lay not in forcing agreement but in cultivating understanding. He refined his approach, tempering his natural ability with patience, his eagerness with precision.

By the time Fisher reached the stage of formal education, he was already miles ahead in understanding the mechanics of argument and influence. His studies would give him structure, would provide the legal framework that would define his career, but his foundation had been built long before he ever set foot in a law classroom. His early life had given him something more valuable than textbook knowledge—it had given him instinct. An intuition for timing, for tone, for the unspoken elements of persuasion that no curriculum could teach.

Every great figure in history is shaped not just by what they learn but by how they learn it. Fisher's path was forged in the unassuming moments that many overlook. It was in the quiet observations of human behavior, in the realization that the true power of words lies not in their volume but in their precision. It was in the understanding that influence is not about dominance but about connection.

The making of Jefferson Fisher did not begin with his first case, nor with his first victory. It began in the earliest days of his life, in the experiences that shaped his voice before he ever knew he would use it to shape the world around him.

CHAPTER 02

The Making of a Lawyer

The transition from a sharp-witted observer to a formidable legal mind was not an overnight phenomenon. Jefferson Fisher's entry into the world of law was a deliberate, calculated move, fueled by his relentless hunger for mastery over language, power, and persuasion. He knew that the courtroom was not just a stage for justice but a battlefield of intellect, where words could mean the difference between triumph and defeat. Every case, every argument, every verdict shaped him into the lawyer he was destined to become.

From the moment he stepped into law school, Fisher was different. While his peers saw their education as a means to a degree, he saw it as a training ground—a place where he could hone the power of persuasion to razor-sharp precision. He did not merely absorb knowledge; he dissected it, questioned it, and wielded it like a sculptor chiseling away imperfections from stone. His ability to analyze case law was not just about memorization; it was about understanding the underlying principles that dictated human behavior and legal outcomes.

In the lecture halls, he was both student and strategist. He listened not just to professors, but to the cadence of their speech, the unspoken cues in their body language, and the ways in which they structured their arguments. He studied not just what was being taught but how it was being delivered. He knew that in law, facts were only half the battle—presentation was everything. And so, he began refining his own delivery, testing the limits of his ability to command a room, to turn skepticism into agreement, to transform complexity into clarity.

Outside of the classroom, Fisher immersed himself in the practical side of law. He sought out mentorships with seasoned attorneys, not content with merely learning the theory—he wanted to witness it in action. He shadowed lawyers in courtrooms, watched their strategies unfold, and took meticulous notes on what worked and what didn't. He volunteered for moot court competitions, treating them not as academic exercises but as opportunities to sharpen his arsenal. With every simulated case, he pushed himself harder, refusing to let even the smallest mistake go uncorrected.

But it was not just the technicalities of law that intrigued him— it was the human element. He was fascinated by the psychology of persuasion, the art of reading a jury, the ability to turn an opponent's strength into a weakness with a well-placed argument. He realized that law was not about winning for the sake of victory; it was about crafting a narrative so compelling that truth and justice became undeniable.

His first real case as a young attorney was not an easy one. The weight of responsibility pressed down on him, the knowledge that a life, a livelihood, or a future could be altered by the words he chose to say. But he did not falter. He prepared relentlessly, pouring over every detail, every precedent, every angle that could be exploited or defended. And when he stepped into that courtroom, he did so not as a novice, but as a force to be reckoned with.

Fisher's approach to law was unlike most. Where others relied on aggression, he relied on control. Where others sought to overpower, he sought to outmaneuver. He understood that the most effective arguments were not the loudest, but the most calculated. He became known for his ability to remain composed under pressure, to dismantle opposing arguments with a precision that left no room for doubt. His opponents often underestimated him, mistaking his calm demeanor for passivity—only to realize, too late, that they had walked into a meticulously laid trap.

With each case, his reputation grew. Clients sought him out not just for his legal acumen, but for his ability to make them feel heard, understood, and protected. He was not just a lawyer; he was an advocate, a strategist, a master of influence. He knew when to press forward and when to hold back, when to let silence speak louder than words. He had refined the art of persuasion into a weapon so potent that even the most difficult cases seemed to tilt in his favor.

As his career progressed, Fisher's impact extended beyond the courtroom. He became a mentor to young attorneys, sharing the insights and strategies that had propelled him to success. He spoke at conferences, breaking down the mechanics of persuasion in ways that resonated with professionals across industries. He understood that the skills he had honed were not just for lawyers—they were for leaders, negotiators, and anyone who sought to command a room with their words.

Yet, despite his success, Fisher never stopped learning. He remained a student of human nature, constantly refining his techniques, analyzing every interaction, and seeking new ways to perfect his craft. He knew that influence was not static; it was an evolving force, shaped by experience, understanding, and an unwavering commitment to mastery.

The making of a lawyer is not defined by a degree or a title—it is defined by the relentless pursuit of excellence, the willingness to adapt, and the ability to turn knowledge into power. Jefferson Fisher embodies this pursuit, a testament to the fact that true influence is not given; it is earned, one word, one argument, and one victory at a time.

CHAPTER 03

The Power of Communication

Jefferson Fisher's ascent into the world of influence was not solely built on intelligence or strategy, but on his unparalleled mastery of communication. Words were never just sounds leaving his lips; they were calculated instruments, fine-tuned to evoke reaction, to shift mindsets, and to command authority. From an early age, he recognized that the difference between success and failure, between winning and losing, often came down to the ability to articulate ideas with clarity, conviction, and precision.

The power of communication is not merely about speaking—it is about understanding. Fisher grasped this principle with an almost instinctive intuition. He saw how people reacted to different tones, how a pause could hold more weight than an entire sentence, how confidence in delivery could make even the most hesitant listener reconsider their stance. This realization transformed his perspective on conversation. Words were not weapons to be wielded recklessly, but tools that, when used correctly, could reshape an entire discussion, a legal battle, or even a life path.

His journey into refining his communication skills was neither accidental nor effortless. It was a process—one that involved meticulous study, relentless practice, and countless failures that taught him valuable lessons. He immersed himself in the great orators of history, dissecting their speeches, analyzing the cadence of their delivery, and internalizing the subtle techniques that made their words unforgettable. From Churchill's steadfast resolve to Obama's measured elegance, from the fiery passion of Martin Luther King Jr. to the cold, calculated precision of legal titans, he learned that there was no singular way to command a room—only the right way for the moment at hand.

Fisher understood that effective communication was not about dominating a conversation, but about guiding it. He mastered the art of listening—not just hearing, but truly absorbing what was being said. He knew that a well-placed silence could unnerve an opponent more than an aggressive retort. He grasped the importance of body language, the weight of a gaze held just long enough, the power of an unwavering stance. The battlefield of discourse was not won with sheer volume or brute rhetoric, but with control—of words, of posture, of presence.

His legal career provided the perfect arena to test and refine these abilities. Every case was an exercise in persuasion, every courtroom a proving ground for the strategies he had honed over the years. He saw firsthand how the slightest inflection in tone could shift a jury's perception, how a measured pause before delivering a key argument could heighten its impact. He recognized that communication was not just about convincing people of what to believe, but about making them feel as though they had arrived at that conclusion themselves. It was a delicate dance—one that required finesse, adaptability, and an almost surgical understanding of human psychology.

Beyond the courtroom, Fisher extended his knowledge to the broader world, understanding that communication was not reserved for legal battles alone. It was the foundation of every relationship, every negotiation, every moment of conflict or resolution. He saw how leaders inspired movements, how individuals defused tension with carefully chosen words, how the simple act of effective communication could dismantle walls that had stood for years. He taught others that influence was not about shouting the loudest, but about speaking in a way that demanded to be heard.

The digital age only amplified the need for mastery over communication. With social media reducing conversations to fleeting soundbites and reactions happening in real-time, the stakes were higher than ever. Fisher adapted, using modern platforms to spread his knowledge, to educate others on the nuances of articulation, composure, and impact. He demonstrated that in a world oversaturated with noise, those who spoke with clarity and intent would always stand out.

His legacy as a communicator was not simply in what he said, but in how he taught others to wield their own voices. He proved that true power did not lie in the ability to argue, but in the ability to connect. To reach people where they were, to shape narratives without coercion, to turn a mere statement into a lasting influence. Jefferson Fisher did not just use communication as a tool—he elevated it to an art form, one that would define his success and cement his influence for generations to come.

CHAPTER 04

Mastering Conflict Resolution

HConflict is one of the most defining forces of human experience. It tests relationships, challenges ideologies, and often stands as the threshold between chaos and order. To master conflict is not merely to settle disputes; it is to harness the very essence of human interaction and wield it with precision, grace, and unshakable control. Few individuals understand this delicate dance as intimately as Jefferson Fisher. His insights into conflict resolution transcend the mundane mechanics of negotiation—they are a profound study of human nature, power dynamics, and the art of persuasion.

Fisher's journey into the realm of conflict resolution did not arise from abstract theory or academic study alone. His understanding is grounded in the visceral, lived realities of human confrontation. From an early age, he grasped the raw power of language—the way a single phrase could cut deeper than a sword, the way a shift in tone could turn hostility into harmony. He understood that true leadership in conflict does not stem from dominance but from an unassailable sense of presence. Through years of navigating legal battles, high-stakes negotiations, and volatile human interactions, Fisher refined his approach into something more than just a method—it became a philosophy.

At the heart of his philosophy is composure, an attribute often undervalued yet essential in the crucible of confrontation. Where others allow emotions to dictate their reactions, Fisher teaches the discipline of restraint. The pause, as he describes it, is not a moment of weakness but a display of supreme control. To pause in the face of provocation is to reclaim power, to shift the dynamic of the exchange. It forces the opposing force to reconsider, to falter, to recognize that they are no longer in control of the emotional current of the conversation. This ability to dictate tempo is the first step toward resolution.

Yet, Fisher's mastery of conflict is not simply about defense—it is also about influence. He dismantles the conventional wisdom that conflict is inherently destructive. Rather, he frames it as an opportunity, a crossroads where one can choose to construct new narratives instead of merely tearing down old ones. Conflict, in his eyes, is a place of transformation. The greatest negotiators, leaders, and strategists understand that the goal is not to win in the conventional sense, but to achieve the outcome that serves the highest purpose.

The tools Fisher employs are not just rhetorical flourishes—they are precise, calculated techniques designed to redirect emotional energy. He reveals how posture alone can shift the trajectory of an argument, how silence can wield more power than the loudest voice in the room. He dissects the psychology of acknowledgment—not as submission, but as a method to de-escalate tension. A nod, a carefully placed phrase, or even a well-timed exhale can unravel aggression and open the door to dialogue.

Fisher's approach extends far beyond professional negotiations or courtroom battles; it seeps into the fabric of everyday life. Whether in business disputes, political confrontations, or personal relationships, his strategies offer a path through the storm. He teaches people to listen—not merely to respond, but to understand. He advocates for clarity, ensuring that words are chosen with intent and precision rather than wielded recklessly as weapons of emotion.

His philosophy is rooted in the belief that conflict is not something to be feared or avoided. It is an essential part of growth, a mechanism through which individuals, organizations, and societies evolve. To master conflict resolution is not just to defuse tensions—it is to command the space where confrontation unfolds, to dictate the rhythm of discourse, and to shape outcomes with intention rather than impulse.

Through his wisdom, Fisher imparts more than just lessons; he hands his audience the keys to a more empowered existence. Those who learn from him do not simply avoid conflict—they control it, mold it, and ultimately use it as a tool for success. In his teachings lies the realization that the power to master conflict is not a rare gift—it is an art, available to all who are willing to study its intricacies, embrace its challenges, and wield its immense potential with precision and purpose.

CHAPTER 05

Building a Social Media Presence

In an age where attention is currency and influence holds more value than gold, mastering the art of social media presence is no longer optional—it is essential. Jefferson Fisher did not merely embrace the digital revolution; he harnessed it, sculpting an online identity that transcended the superficiality of likes and followers. His digital footprint is a testament to strategy, authenticity, and an acute understanding of human psychology. To build a social media presence is not simply to post content— it is to cultivate a brand, to craft a persona, and to command a space where millions converge in search of direction, inspiration, and engagement.

Fisher's journey into the digital world was not born out of vanity or the need for validation. It was a deliberate choice, a tactical maneuver designed to extend his reach far beyond the courtroom. He understood that social media is not just a platform but a stage—a global amphitheater where the most compelling voices dictate the narrative of their industry. With an unwavering commitment to value-driven content, he positioned himself not as an influencer in the conventional sense but as a thought leader, a digital architect of wisdom who transformed the way audiences perceive conflict resolution, communication, and personal empowerment.

At the core of his digital mastery lies authenticity. Unlike many who succumb to the temptations of curated perfection, Fisher embraced imperfection as a strength. His presence is not dictated by scripts but by raw, unfiltered connection. He speaks not to an audience but with them, bridging the gap between virtual and real-life influence. His digital presence is a mirror of his professional ethos—direct, impactful, and unwaveringly genuine. Every post, every video, every interaction is crafted with intent, not merely to engage but to educate and inspire.

Fisher's approach to social media is rooted in a deep understanding of audience psychology. He does not merely create content; he engineers it. He deciphers the nuances of engagement, recognizing that attention spans are fleeting and that relevance is earned, not given. His mastery of platform algorithms, content trends, and audience behavior allows him to maintain a dynamic presence that evolves with the digital landscape. He recognizes that virality is not accidental—it is a calculated result of precision, timing, and the ability to evoke emotion.

Beyond strategy, Fisher's digital dominance is a product of consistency. Many falter in the realm of social media not due to lack of talent but due to inconsistency. Fisher understands that presence is built not overnight but over time, through relentless dedication to providing value. Whether through thought-provoking insights, compelling storytelling, or interactive discussions, he ensures that his audience remains engaged, connected, and invested in his journey.

Perhaps the most profound aspect of Fisher's social media presence is his ability to translate digital influence into real-world impact. He does not exist within the confines of a screen; he uses his platform as a bridge, connecting ideas to action, theory to practice. His followers do not simply consume his content; they embody it, applying his wisdom to their own lives, careers, and relationships. He is not just a content creator; he is a catalyst for transformation.

Building a social media presence is not about accumulating followers—it is about cultivating a community. Fisher's digital empire is not measured by numbers but by the depth of impact. His audience is not passive but engaged, not transient but loyal. They do not merely watch; they listen, learn, and evolve. His influence extends beyond screens, embedding itself into the very fabric of personal and professional development for those who seek to master the art of communication, leadership, and resilience.

The power of social media lies not in its technology but in its ability to amplify voices, to democratize influence, and to reshape the world in real-time. Fisher stands as a testament to what can be achieved when social media is wielded with intelligence, integrity, and purpose. His journey is a blueprint for anyone seeking to carve their digital legacy—not through gimmicks or fleeting trends but through the timeless power of authenticity, strategy, and relentless value creation.

CHAPTER 06

The Art of Handling Difficult Conversations

Difficult conversations are an inevitable part of life. They emerge in boardrooms, courtrooms, living rooms, and across dinner tables. They arise in the professional world, where high-stakes negotiations determine the trajectory of careers and companies, and in personal relationships, where words possess the power to heal or irreparably wound. The ability to handle these conversations with skill, tact, and emotional intelligence is one of the most valuable yet elusive competencies one can master. Jefferson Fisher has not only demonstrated a remarkable aptitude for navigating such exchanges but has also illuminated a path for others to follow, offering tools to approach even the most contentious discussions with confidence, clarity, and control.

At the heart of Fisher's approach lies preparation—not just of arguments and counterpoints, but of mindset and emotional state. Many individuals approach difficult conversations in a reactive state, driven by emotions, defense mechanisms, and a need to win. Fisher dismantles this flawed approach, replacing it with one rooted in strategy, self-awareness, and the profound understanding that the purpose of a conversation is not always to emerge victorious, but to emerge enlightened, connected, and with forward momentum. He emphasizes the importance of knowing one's objectives before stepping into the conversational arena, distinguishing between what is essential and what is expendable in discourse.

Composure is the cornerstone of his philosophy. Fisher's command of difficult conversations is not predicated on overpowering his counterpart but on maintaining control over himself. The ability to stay calm amid tension, to slow the rhythm of discourse when emotions escalate, and to refrain from the immediate impulse to react defines his methodology. He teaches that silence, when used intentionally, can be more powerful than words, forcing the other party to fill the space, often revealing more than they intended. Through careful listening, he unearths the true motivations behind statements, recognizing that surface-level expressions often conceal deeper fears, needs, and desires.

Another pillar of his technique is the ability to frame conversations constructively. Fisher has mastered the art of reframing—shifting perspectives in a way that transforms adversarial interactions into collaborative dialogues. He understands that people are more likely to respond positively when they feel heard and valued. This is where validation becomes a transformative tool. Fisher does not equate validation with agreement; instead, he utilizes it as a mechanism to de-escalate tension and create an environment conducive to progress. By acknowledging emotions and perspectives, he diffuses hostility and fosters an atmosphere where resolution becomes possible.

The art of handling difficult conversations also requires an astute awareness of language. Words can be weapons or bridges, and

Fisher wields them with precision. He avoids absolutes, knowing that words like "always" and "never" breed defensiveness. Instead, he utilizes open-ended questions, allowing conversations to flow organically while subtly steering them toward productive outcomes. His ability to identify and neutralize triggers before they escalate is a skill honed through years of high-pressure negotiations and emotionally charged discussions.

Beyond techniques and strategies, Fisher's approach is underscored by a deep commitment to integrity. He recognizes that difficult conversations often test one's moral compass, tempting individuals to manipulate, deceive, or exploit vulnerabilities. Yet, true mastery lies in maintaining ethical clarity even in the most challenging exchanges. He advocates for honesty, transparency, and fairness, understanding that long-term credibility far outweighs short-term victories.

Perhaps one of the most compelling aspects of Fisher's teachings is his belief in the transformative potential of difficult conversations. Rather than viewing them as obstacles, he sees them as opportunities—opportunities to learn, to connect, to grow. A conversation that once seemed insurmountable can become a turning point, a catalyst for change, a moment where understanding triumphs over division.

Jefferson Fisher does not merely teach people how to handle difficult conversations; he equips them with the mindset and mastery to thrive within them. He imparts the wisdom that words, when wielded with intention, are among the most powerful tools at one's disposal. Through his insights, individuals gain not just the ability to navigate challenging dialogues, but the confidence to step into them with purpose, skill, and unwavering composure.

CHAPTER 07

The Business of Influence

Influence is not merely a byproduct of expertise—it is a currency, a force that shapes industries, defines careers, and molds public perception. Jefferson Fisher has not only cultivated influence but has strategically harnessed it to create business opportunities that extend far beyond his foundational expertise. His journey exemplifies how mastery in a field, when coupled with a keen understanding of human psychology and market dynamics, can be transformed into a thriving enterprise.

Fisher's rise to prominence did not occur in isolation; it was fueled by an acute awareness of how perception drives opportunity. His command over communication, conflict resolution, and negotiation positioned him as a figure of authority, but it was his ability to translate these skills into actionable business ventures that set him apart. Understanding that visibility equates to viability, he leveraged platforms beyond traditional legal and professional spheres to amplify his reach. His voice was not confined to courtrooms or conference rooms— it extended into digital spaces, media engagements, and industry think tanks, where his insights became indispensable.

The evolution of his influence into a business empire did not happen by chance. Fisher recognized early on that expertise alone does not guarantee success; it must be packaged, marketed, and delivered in ways that resonate with the right audience. He mastered the art of storytelling, crafting narratives that engaged not only clients but broader audiences hungry for knowledge, guidance, and inspiration. Whether through keynote speeches, online courses, workshops, or consultancy, he built an ecosystem where his knowledge became a sought-after commodity.

One of the cornerstones of his success was his ability to adapt. In a rapidly shifting digital landscape, Fisher did not remain tethered to antiquated methods of influence. Instead, he embraced emerging trends, harnessing the power of social media, digital branding, and content marketing to expand his presence. He understood that engagement was the new metric of authority and that to remain relevant, one must not only provide value but also foster community. By developing online platforms where individuals could interact with his teachings, he transformed passive audiences into active participants in his brand.

Monetization of influence is an art, and Fisher's approach was both strategic and ethical. He did not commodify his expertise at the expense of integrity; rather, he built business ventures rooted in value-driven leadership. Through mentorship programs, executive coaching, and proprietary training methodologies, he ensured that those who invested in his guidance received tangible results. His ability to distill complex concepts into actionable strategies made his teachings applicable across industries, attracting corporate executives, entrepreneurs, and professionals eager to refine their own skills of influence.

His influence extended beyond his own brand. Fisher became a consultant for businesses, institutions, and policymakers seeking to navigate the intricacies of negotiation, crisis management, and public relations. His insights proved invaluable in shaping organizational cultures, refining leadership strategies, and developing communication frameworks that optimized both internal and external interactions. By bridging the gap between theory and practice, he carved a niche where his expertise became indispensable.

The business of influence also requires an understanding of scalability. Fisher's ventures were not limited to one-on-one engagements; he developed scalable business models that allowed his expertise to reach larger audiences without diluting its impact. From licensing his methodologies to corporations to creating digital courses that democratized access to his teachings, he expanded his reach while maintaining the quality of his message.

Yet, influence is not just about business—it is about legacy. Fisher's long-term vision extended beyond revenue generation; he aimed to cultivate a lasting impact, shaping the future of leadership and communication. By fostering networks of professionals who could implement and pass on his teachings, he ensured that his influence would ripple through generations. He understood that true success is not measured merely in financial gain but in the enduring value one leaves behind.

Jefferson Fisher's expertise, when paired with strategic execution, became more than just a skill set—it became a movement. His ability to translate influence into opportunity is a testament to the power of mastery, adaptability, and ethical leadership. He has not only built a business; he has redefined what it means to wield influence with purpose, precision, and unwavering integrity.

CHAPTER 08

Leadership Lessons from the Courtroom

The courtroom is a crucible where leadership is tested, sharpened, and ultimately defined. It is a theater of human emotion, a battlefield of wits, and a proving ground for those who seek to command with presence, clarity, and strategy. Jefferson Fisher, having navigated the high-stakes world of litigation, emerged not only as a formidable attorney but as a leader whose insights extend far beyond legal walls. The lessons forged in the heat of trial advocacy are ones that resonate with entrepreneurs, executives, politicians, and anyone aspiring to lead with decisiveness and wisdom.

Leadership in the courtroom is about more than just persuasion; it is about commanding respect, managing crisis, and executing under pressure. The adversarial nature of litigation places a premium on composure, a trait that defines Fisher's approach to leadership. The ability to remain unshaken amid chaos, to respond rather than react, to absorb pressure without buckling—these are qualities that separate exceptional leaders from the rest. Control over one's emotions is not a weakness; it is the armor that protects decision-making from the distortions of fear and frustration.

One of the most vital lessons drawn from the courtroom is the power of preparation. No great trial attorney walks into court unarmed with knowledge, research, and strategy. Leadership, much like advocacy, is built upon the foundation of meticulous preparation. The leaders who inspire confidence are those who anticipate challenges before they arise, who craft contingencies with the foresight of a grandmaster in chess. Fisher's career is a testament to the idea that thorough preparation is not an option— it is the price of entry for success.

Yet, even the most prepared leader must be adaptable. Trials are unpredictable, much like the broader world of business and governance. Witnesses deviate from expected testimony, judges rule unexpectedly, and opposing counsel introduces unforeseen arguments. The ability to pivot without losing focus is a skill honed through experience, one that allows a leader to maintain authority even when circumstances shift. Fisher's career exemplifies this balance between preparation and flexibility, showcasing how true leadership is the mastery of both structure and spontaneity.

Another hallmark of great leadership is the art of communication. The most brilliant legal argument is useless if it cannot be conveyed with clarity, persuasion, and resonance. In the courtroom, language is both sword and shield. Every word carries weight, every pause holds meaning, and every statement is an opportunity to sway minds. Fisher understood that effective leaders are not those who merely talk, but those who make people listen. The ability to distill complex ideas into digestible, compelling narratives is a defining trait of influential figures in any field.

Integrity is another cornerstone of courtroom leadership. While tactics and strategy play a role in trial advocacy, credibility is the ultimate currency. A lawyer who loses the trust of the judge, jury, or client is a lawyer who has forfeited their greatest asset. The same principle applies to leadership in any arena. Leaders who compromise their integrity for short-term gains inevitably erode their own authority. Fisher's approach to legal practice reinforced the idea that leadership is not merely about winning—it is about winning the right way.

Empathy, often overlooked in traditional leadership discussions, is a trait that Fisher wielded with precision. The best trial attorneys are those who understand human nature, who can step into the minds of jurors, opposing counsel, and clients to navigate the intricacies of perception and decision-making. Leadership requires a similar level of emotional intelligence. Those who lead effectively do not do so through sheer force of will but through a deep understanding of the motivations, fears, and aspirations of those they guide. The courtroom taught Fisher that true influence is built upon the ability to connect on a human level.

Crisis management is another dimension of leadership that finds its most intense training ground in the courtroom. Unexpected developments can shift the trajectory of a trial within moments, demanding immediate and decisive action. The courtroom does not grant the luxury of hesitation—leaders must make judgment calls with conviction. The ability to operate under extreme pressure, to make split-second decisions with confidence, and to rally a team through turbulent moments is an invaluable skill for any leader, and one that Fisher mastered through experience.

Beyond individual performance, leadership in the courtroom is also about teamwork. Even the most brilliant attorneys rely on a network of paralegals, co-counsel, investigators, and clerks to construct a case. Delegation, trust, and collaboration are critical components of success. Leaders who attempt to shoulder every burden alone inevitably collapse under the weight of responsibility. Fisher's career serves as a reminder that great leaders empower those around them, recognizing that collective strength far surpasses individual effort.

Ultimately, the courtroom is a mirror that reflects the true essence of leadership. It exposes weaknesses, highlights strengths, and demands constant evolution. Fisher's journey through litigation provided him with lessons that transcend the legal field, offering a blueprint for those who seek to lead with wisdom, resilience, and ethical conviction. His experiences illustrate that leadership is not an inherent trait but a cultivated discipline—one that requires practice, patience, and an unwavering commitment to growth.

Jefferson Fisher did not merely emerge from the courtroom as a successful attorney; he emerged as a leader whose insights now guide individuals far beyond the legal profession. His story underscores that the principles of advocacy, preparation, communication, and integrity are not confined to legal battles but are the very bedrock upon which great leadership is built.

CHAPTER 09

Navigating Controversy and Criticism

Controversy and criticism are inevitable for those who dare to step into the limelight. They are the sharp edges of influence, the price one pays for visibility and power. For Jefferson Fisher, these forces have been both adversaries and teachers, shaping his path and refining his approach to leadership, communication, and resilience.

A man who speaks with conviction will always invite scrutiny. It is the nature of discourse, the cost of challenging norms, and the reality of wielding influence in a world where opinions clash like waves against a rocky shore. Fisher, however, does not flinch in the face of opposition. He embraces it, understanding that within criticism lies an opportunity to sharpen his message, refine his approach, and, at times, prove his detractors wrong not with aggression but with unshakable poise.

Criticism, when examined closely, often reveals more about the critic than the one being judged. Some attack out of misunderstanding, some from envy, and others from a desire to defend their own beliefs. Fisher understands this deeply and responds not with immediate retaliation but with strategic patience. He listens, absorbs, and evaluates before deciding whether a response is necessary. He recognizes that every battle does not need to be fought, that silence can sometimes be the most disarming weapon, and that a well-placed response carries more weight than a flurry of reactive words.

Throughout his career, Fisher has faced numerous controversies—some manufactured, some legitimate. What sets him apart is his ability to navigate these storms without losing his core identity. He remains steadfast in his beliefs while adapting his tactics to fit the landscape of the debate. His philosophy is simple: control the narrative, never let emotions dictate responses, and always operate from a foundation of integrity.

Social media, a double-edged sword, has amplified both his reach and the scrutiny he faces. In an era where digital outrage can spread like wildfire, Fisher has mastered the art of digital discourse. He does not engage in petty online feuds, nor does he allow baseless accusations to shake his confidence. Instead, he uses the very platforms that others attempt to weaponize against him to further his mission, turning controversy into content, criticism into conversation, and opposition into engagement.

For every detractor, there are countless supporters who see through the noise and recognize authenticity. Fisher does not seek universal approval—such a pursuit is futile. Instead, he focuses on those who are willing to listen, learn, and engage in meaningful dialogue. He believes that influence is not about silencing opposition but about standing firm in the face of it, about responding with wisdom rather than impulse, and about proving one's worth through consistent action rather than defensive words.

His approach to controversy is not just about survival—it is about mastery. He does not merely weather storms; he learns from them, adapts to them, and, ultimately, uses them to propel himself forward. Every criticism, every attack, and every challenge is an opportunity to refine his craft, reinforce his values, and strengthen his legacy. Jefferson Fisher does not fear controversy. He owns it, navigates it, and emerges from it stronger than before.

CHAPTER 10

The Future of Persuasion and Influence

Persuasion and influence have long been the undercurrents that shape societies, drive movements, and determine the rise and fall of leaders. As the world moves deeper into an era dominated by rapid technological advancements, evolving communication landscapes, and shifting cultural paradigms, the future of persuasion and influence stands on the precipice of transformation. Jefferson Fisher, a master of communication and an astute observer of human behavior, recognizes that the principles of persuasion are not static relics of the past but living, evolving forces that adapt with time.

The digital age has redefined the art of influence. Where once persuasion relied on rhetoric in public squares or boardrooms, today's battlefield stretches across multiple digital platforms, each with its own set of rules, algorithms, and audiences. The ability to wield influence is no longer confined to a select few— it is democratized, accessible to anyone who understands the mechanics of digital engagement. Fisher foresees a future where persuasion is less about authority and more about authenticity, where influence is not dictated by hierarchy but by relatability, and where the most effective communicators are those who foster genuine connections in an increasingly fragmented world.

Artificial intelligence and machine learning have begun to play an unprecedented role in shaping human perception. Algorithms dictate what people see, hear, and engage with, subtly guiding opinions and behaviors in ways never before possible. The challenge of the future will not only be about mastering the art of communication but also about navigating the invisible forces that shape digital discourse. Fisher believes that the key to sustaining influence in this evolving landscape lies in ethical persuasion— leveraging technology not as a manipulative tool but as a bridge to understanding, connection, and meaningful dialogue.

The rise of misinformation and deepfake technology poses another significant challenge to the future of influence. As artificial content generation blurs the line between reality and fabrication, trust becomes an even more valuable currency. Fisher predicts that persuasion will rely less on spectacle and more on credibility. Those who can cultivate and maintain trust will hold the power, while those who engage in deception will find their influence fleeting. In this new era, transparency and consistency will be the pillars upon which lasting persuasion is built.

Human psychology remains the cornerstone of persuasion, even as the tools change. The principles of emotional resonance, storytelling, and strategic framing will endure, but their application will become more intricate. Fisher anticipates a future where successful influencers will need to master not just verbal and written communication but also the language of data, visuals, and immersive experiences. The convergence of communication and technology will demand a new breed of persuaders—those who can blend traditional rhetorical skills with digital fluency.

The evolution of influence also extends to leadership. The leaders of tomorrow will not simply command; they will engage, inspire, and adapt. Fisher envisions a shift from rigid authority to dynamic leadership, where persuasion is an ongoing dialogue rather than a one-sided declaration. The ability to listen, synthesize information, and articulate compelling narratives will define the most effective leaders in business, politics, and social movements.

The future of persuasion and influence is a vast, ever-changing landscape, filled with both challenges and opportunities. Jefferson Fisher's insights provide a roadmap for those who wish to navigate this terrain with skill and integrity. The power of persuasion is no longer about dominance—it is about resonance, connection, and the ability to shape ideas in a way that fosters real impact. As technology advances, as human interactions evolve, and as the very nature of influence transforms, those who embrace change with clarity, purpose, and ethical intent will not only survive but thrive in the world of tomorrow.

CONCLUSION

Legacies are not built in a day, nor are they measured solely by the milestones of a single lifetime. They are woven into the fabric of history, shaped by the influence exerted, the lives touched, and the ideas that outlive their creators. Jefferson Fisher's legacy is not merely a reflection of his success in law, communication, and influence—it is a testament to the transformative power of words and the profound impact of ethical persuasion. His name will not just be remembered; it will resonate in the minds of those who seek to understand the art of connection, the science of influence, and the moral compass that guides true leadership.

At the heart of Fisher's enduring influence is his ability to decode human interaction with unparalleled precision. His expertise extends far beyond the courtroom, seeping into everyday conversations, professional negotiations, and public discourse. By distilling complex psychological principles into practical, actionable strategies, he has revolutionized the way people engage, debate, and resolve conflicts. His methods are not abstract theories confined to academic settings; they are tangible tools that individuals from all walks of life can wield to navigate their personal and professional worlds.

The digital revolution has given rise to an unprecedented era of global communication, where ideas travel faster than ever, and narratives shape entire generations. Fisher's teachings serve as a guiding light in this evolving landscape, ensuring that the principles of ethical persuasion remain intact amidst a sea of manipulation, misinformation, and digital chaos. His work has emphasized that influence is not about deception but about clarity, integrity, and the power of authentic storytelling. He has shown that true persuasion is not a tool of coercion but an art form that, when wielded with responsibility, can unite, inspire, and elevate societies.

Fisher's presence in the legal arena was not just defined by his victories but by the way he conducted himself—an unwavering commitment to fairness, an unshakeable belief in justice, and an unrelenting drive to bring resolution where conflict reigned. His courtroom prowess was never about theatrics or empty rhetoric; it was about precision, strategy, and a deep understanding of human nature. He mastered the delicate balance of logic and emotion, proving time and again that the most persuasive argument is one rooted in truth.

But his influence stretches far beyond the legal profession. As a thought leader in the realm of communication, Fisher has left an indelible mark on the corporate world, the digital sphere, and the countless individuals who have sought his wisdom. His guidance has reshaped leadership structures, helping executives, entrepreneurs, and influencers refine their voices and amplify their impact. His legacy is found in boardrooms where negotiations take a more constructive turn, in political debates where integrity holds more weight than aggression, and in social interactions where understanding replaces hostility.

His teachings on conflict resolution remain a cornerstone of his legacy. The world is fraught with discord—between nations, within organizations, and among individuals. Fisher's insights provide a blueprint for dismantling tension, encouraging dialogue, and fostering reconciliation. His belief that communication is the bridge between division and unity has inspired a new generation of problem-solvers, leaders, and visionaries who strive to mend the fractures in society.

Perhaps one of the most remarkable aspects of Fisher's legacy is the way it continues to evolve. Unlike statues that stand motionless in tribute, his impact is fluid, continuously shaping and adapting to new challenges, new voices, and new mediums of influence. His presence in the digital world ensures that his lessons are not relics of the past but living, breathing principles that guide current and future generations. Through online platforms, educational initiatives, and ongoing mentorship, his voice remains alive, urging people to master the art of persuasion with conscience and care.

A true measure of a legacy is its ability to inspire those who follow. Fisher's influence has not only empowered individuals to become better communicators but has also ignited a movement— a call to embrace ethical persuasion as a means of transformation rather than manipulation. His name is synonymous with wisdom in communication, but more importantly, it is a symbol of the responsibility that comes with influence. To persuade is to hold power, and to hold power is to bear an obligation to wield it ethically.

As time progresses, the echoes of Jefferson Fisher's teachings will continue to reverberate in courtrooms, lecture halls, corporate offices, and digital platforms alike. His work is a beacon for those seeking to bridge divides, foster understanding, and make a lasting impact on the world. He has proven that words, when used with precision and integrity, can move mountains, shape futures, and carve legacies that withstand the test of time.

Jefferson Fisher's story does not conclude with the turning of these pages. His legacy lives on in the countless individuals he has influenced, the minds he has sharpened, and the conversations he has changed. The world will continue to seek guidance from his words, drawing strength from his principles and inspiration from his unwavering dedication to the art of persuasion. And so, his legacy endures—not as a distant memory, but as an ever-present force shaping the communicators, leaders, and visionaries of tomorrow.

JEFFERSON FISHER

"THE ART OF INFLUENCE"

"Mastering Communication, Leadership, and Persuasion in the Modern Age"

ZAHRA REHAN

Made in United States
Orlando, FL
22 March 2025